Copyright under USMC protection

The Betide cottage, one of Earl Young's stone houses.

Published by: Boulder Press, P.O. Box 1583, Solana Beach, CA 92075

Photography and Text © 2014 Mike Barton. Photographer's website: www.mikebartonphoto.com

Individual prints may be purchased directly from the photographer: cell phone (720) 934-4322

No part of this book may be reproduced in any form without written permission from the publisher.

Editor: David L. Miles, Co-director, Harsha House Museum, Charlevoix (Michigan) Historical Society

Library of Congress Control Number: 2014903074

ISBN 13: 978-0-9899268-1-2
Second Edition: 2014
Created and designed in the United States
Printed in China

Charlevoix
the Beautiful II

photography and text by Mike Barton
foreword David L. Miles

BOULDER PRESS

59 Charlevoix Lighthouse	106 Beyond Charlevoix
67 Beaches	113 About the Photographer

CHARLEVOIX HAVE FUN OR DON'T

Foreword

Charlevoix, Michigan has long been celebrated as one of the most memorable towns to be found anywhere, known by many across the United States and abroad. Once the two channels that connect inland Lake Charlevoix to Lake Michigan via central Round Lake were cut in 1869, the world has beaten a pathway to its door. The first permanent settlers of what was called Pine River, until the official name change of 1879, arrived in 1854 to escape religious despotism. Fishermen followed, then the lumbering business in the 1860s. As more and more people began to discover its charms, word spread nationwide. The resort and tourism industry began to blossom in the late 1870s. By the time the railroad arrived in 1892, Charlevoix had firmly established itself as one of the premier vacation destinations in the Midwest, with guests arriving from both coasts. The town's unique configurations on three lakes and eleven shorelines have welcomed millions of visitors over 160 years to what many mariners have long regarded as the finest naturally protected harbor on the Great Lakes.

A longtime visitor, Mike Barton has turned his expert eye on the town for the second time and captured anew the essence of Charlevoix in the remarkable color images contained within these pages. Rarely has this beautiful town received such glowing tribute as it has in *Charlevoix the Beautiful II*.

David L. Miles 2014
Co-director, Harsha House Museum
Charlevoix Historical Society

CHARLEVOIX THE BEAUTIFUL II

Introduction

Nestled between Lake Michigan and Round Lake lies the charming northern Michigan town known as "Charlevoix the Beautiful." Located near the "Tip of the Mitt," Charlevoix is a popular summer destination for travelers from all over the world. Crowds swell and fade away. They come for a day, a week, the season. Some never leave.

In addition to its picturesque setting and friendly small town atmosphere, Charlevoix features art galleries, concert performances, festivals and of course shopping while enjoying a piece of fudge or two.

Families flock to the beaches to sunbathe, swim or simply enjoy the rhythmic sound of waves washing ashore, for you are never far from a beach in Charlevoix.

Decorative baskets overflowing with colorful flowers hang from downtown lampposts throughout the summer. The huge terraced waterfront park spills down to the Round Lake Yacht Basin. It's no wonder Forbes named it one of "America's Prettiest Towns" and Yachting magazine hailed it as the second "Best Waterfront Town in the World."

Charlevoix is one of the few remaining towns with an operating drawbridge, a spectacle that fascinates visitors as it opens to let yachts and sailboats travel

ABOVE: The ferry *Emerald Isle II* returns to Charlevoix after a two hour, 32-mile journey from Beaver Island.
OPPOSITE PAGE: Colorful Bridge Street is the town's hub of activity.

between Lake Michigan and Round Lake. And the local Mushroom Houses, the stone creations of Earl Young, are known world-wide and the only place you can see them is in Charlevoix.

The name "Charlevoix" comes from Pierre Francois Xavier de Charlevoix, a French priest who visited the area in 1721 when exploring the Great Lakes. At the time, Native Americans lived along the lakeshore Pine River bluffs near where the lighthouse is today.

Fishermen began to come to the Pine River area in the mid 1800s. But in 1853, tensions between the fishermen and the Mormons of Beaver Island led to the Battle of Pine River. It is claimed to be the only battle on the Great Lakes fought on both land and sea.

Shortly after the battle, fishermen abandoned the Pine River for a less hostile environment. In 1854 a Mormon family disillusioned with the violent, authoritarian life they found on Beaver Island retreated to the mainland where they established Charlevoix's first permanent homestead in a settlement abandoned a year earlier by the fishermen who where fearful of island retribution.

From sailing or a round of golf to the simple pleasures of a walk along the beach or just watching the sunset over Lake Michigan, this harborside town has a charm of its own. There are two kinds of people who visit Charlevoix, those who will return and those who wish they could.

INTRODUCTION

PAGE 10: Halfway to the Top is a clothing store on Bridge Street. Charlevoix is located just north of the 45th parallel (latitude 45) or halfway to the North Pole from the equator.

ABOVE AND OPPOSITE PAGE: East Park and the Round Lake marina went through a massive renovation from 2007-2009 and were named one of America's Ten Best Public Spaces by the American Planning Association in 2009.

RIGHT: Odmark Performance Pavilion. The lakeside amphitheater in East Park is host to the Summer Concert Series.

ABOVE: The *Falcon*, one of John Cross Fisheries' trap-netter tugs, races home through the Pine River Channel after a morning on Lake Michigan. Every day, the tiny weather-beaten boat brings in a fresh catch of salmon, perch and walleye, lake trout and of course whitefish.

LEFT: The Weathervane Inn Restaurant (front) and Weathervane Terrace Inn motel (rear left) were designed by legendary builder Earl Young.

GREAT LAKES SAILING CO.
SAILING SPOKEN HERE
BAREFOOT CRUISES
WELCOME ABOARD

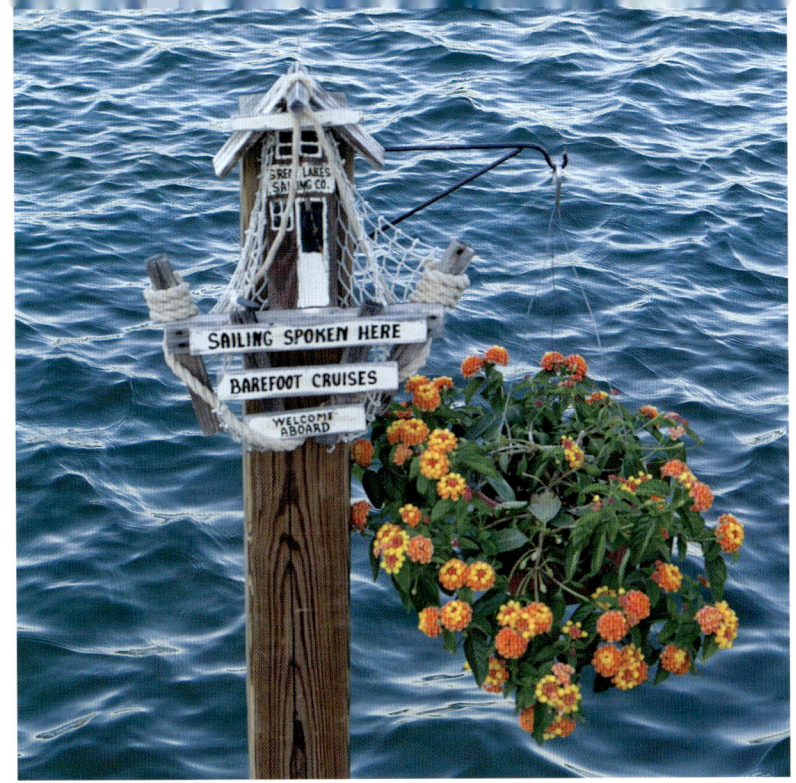

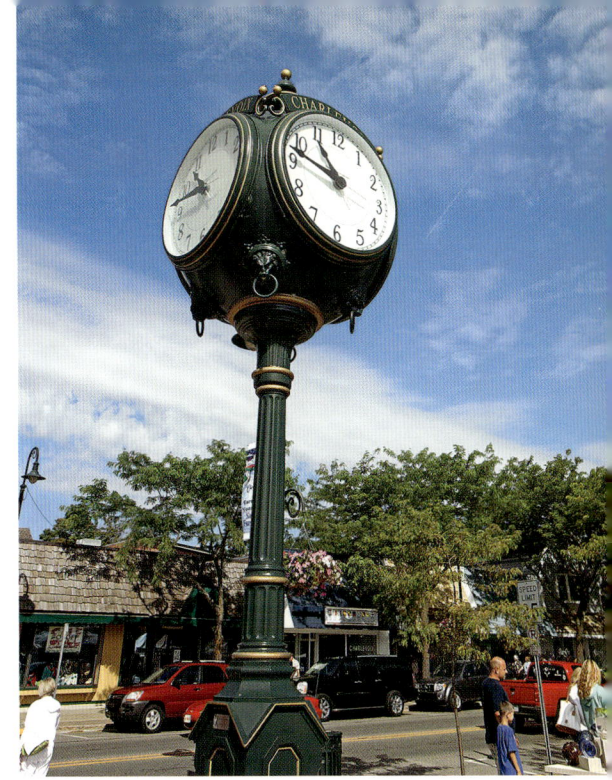

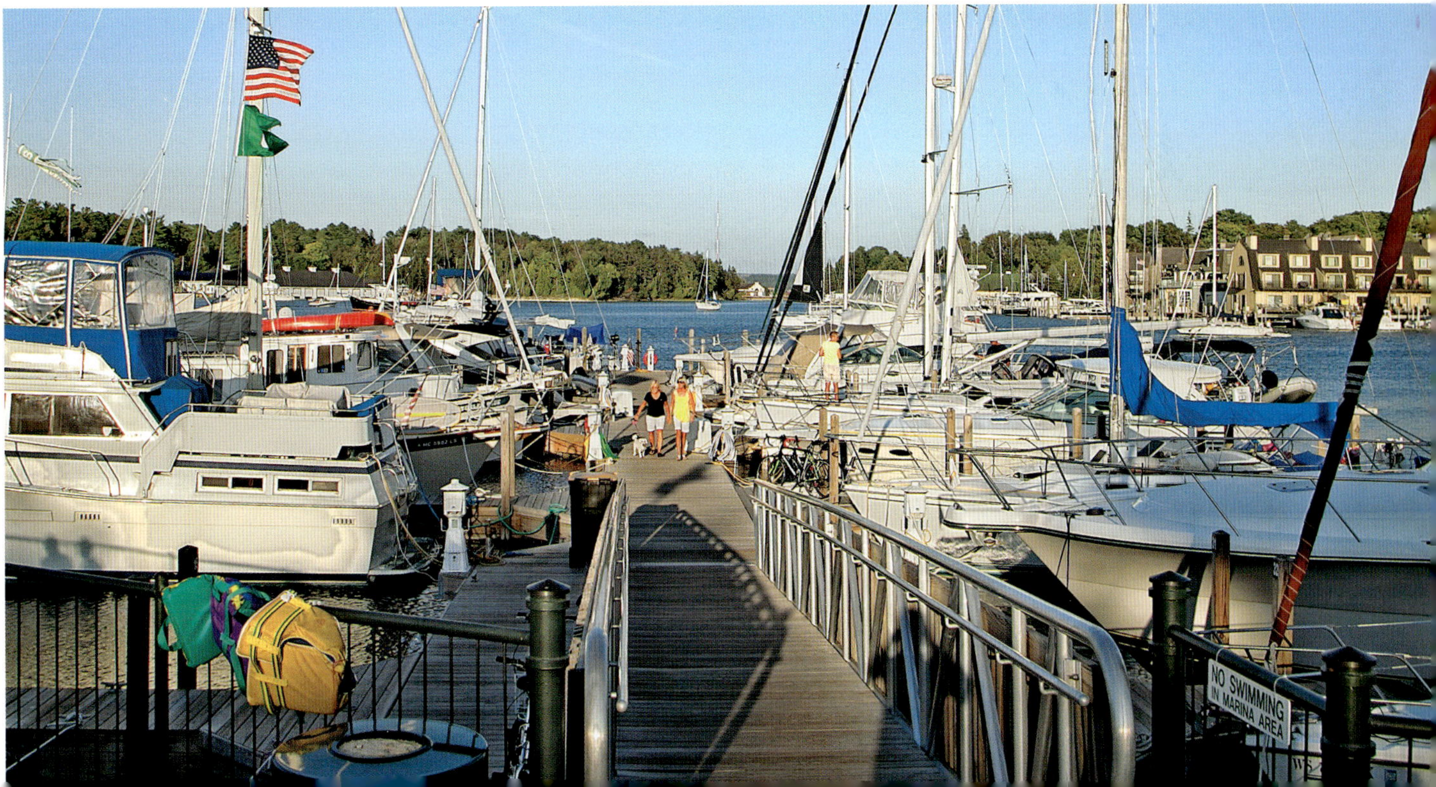
NO SWIMMING IN MARINA AREA

ABOVE: A crew member of the schooner *Inland Seas*. Through its educational shipboard programs, the Inland Seas Education Association gives people of all ages the opportunity to experience the Great Lakes firsthand.

ABOVE: Passenger service to the Charlevoix Train Depot ended in 1962. The station was donated to the Charlevoix Historical Society in June 1992 on the 100th anniversary of the first train arriving in Charlevoix. After being restored, the depot now serves as a meeting place for history programs, special exhibits, and social events.
OPPOSITE PAGE CLOCKWISE: The Charlevoix United Methodist Church (1878), Christ Episcopal Church (1894), the view from the top of a tiny ski hill at Mount McSauba Park, and the buoy marking the entrance to the Harbour Club condominium.

RIGHT: Buoy tending and Coast Guard stations have served Charlevoix since 1898. Station Charlevoix, as it is officially known, was originally located near the lighthouse before moving to its present site in the mid 1960s near the inlet between Lake Charlevoix and Round Lake.

The *Spencer F. Baird* is a research and fish stocking ship named after a renowned zoologist. The Fish and Wildlife Service utilizes the 95-feet-long, 30-feet-wide vessel to release about 3.7 million lake trout into the Great Lakes annually. In 1871, Ulysses S. Grant appointed Baird as the first commissioner of the U.S. Fish and Fisheries Commission.

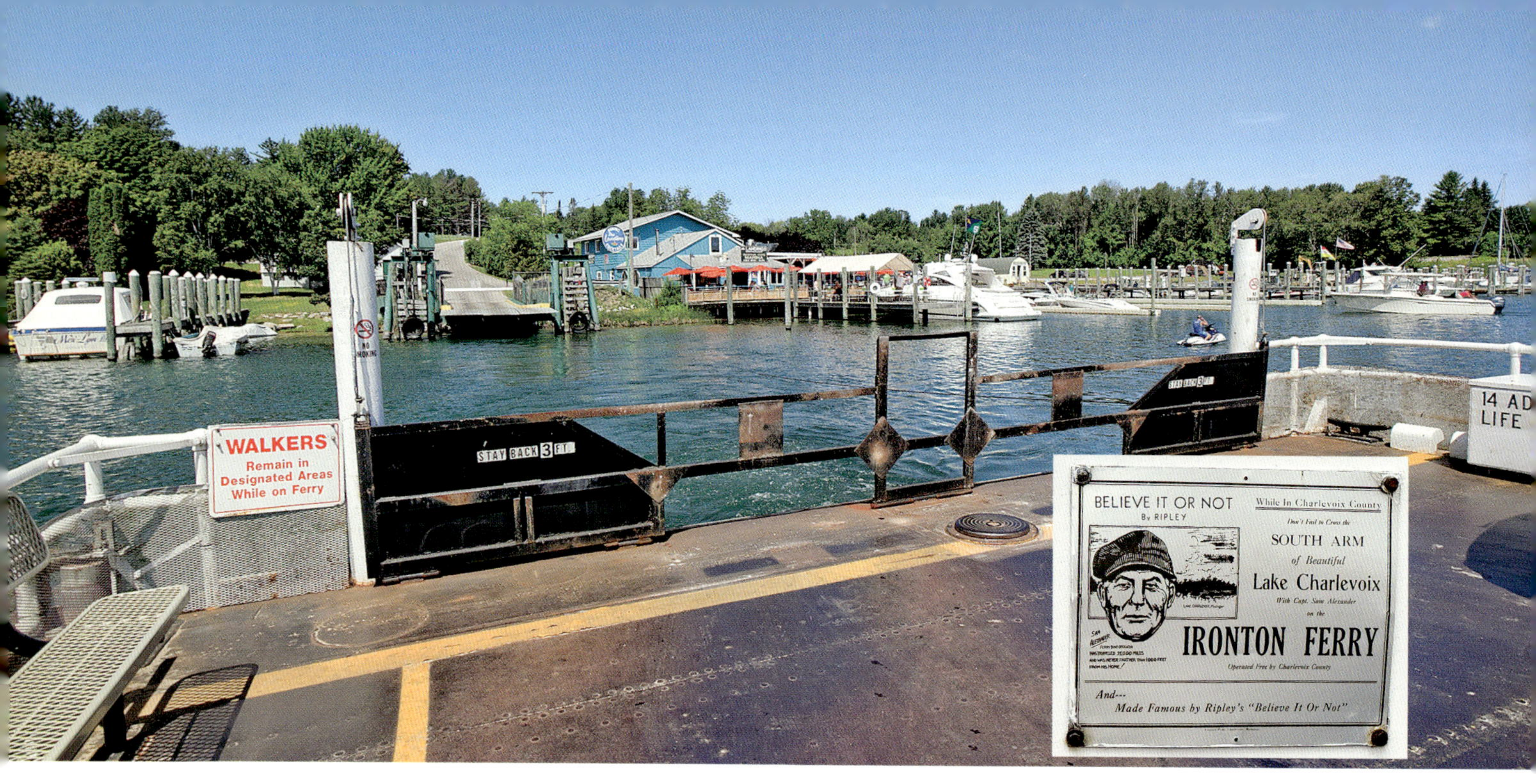
WALKERS
Remain in Designated Areas While on Ferry
STAY BACK 3 FT.
BELIEVE IT OR NOT
By RIPLEY
While In Charlevoix County
Don't Fail to Cross the
SOUTH ARM
of Beautiful
Lake Charlevoix
With Capt. Sam Alexander
on the
IRONTON FERRY
Operated Free by Charlevoix County
And---
Made Famous by Ripley's "Believe It Or Not"

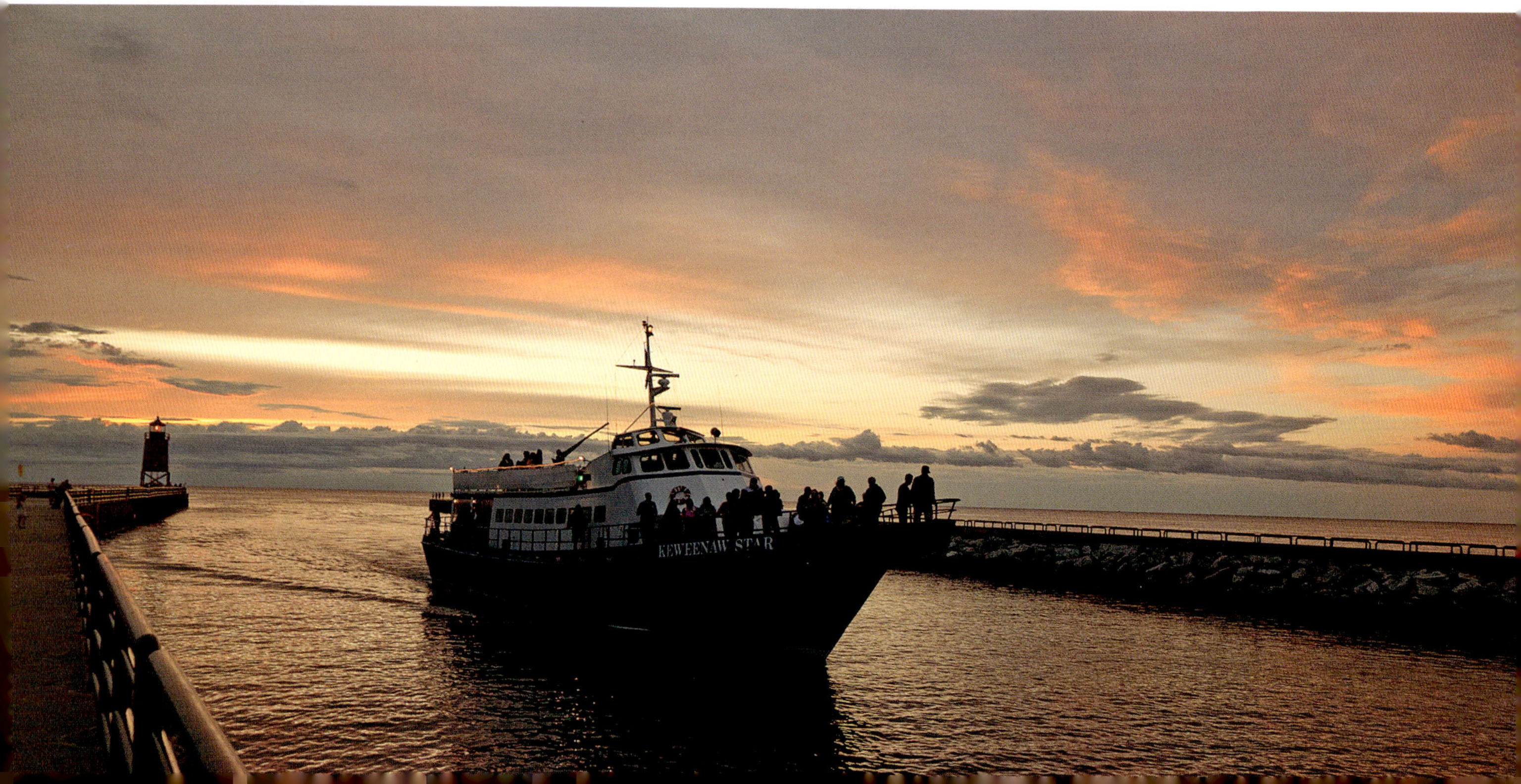
KEWEENAW STAR

OPPOSITE PAGE TOP: The Ironton Ferry makes about 100 trips across the South Arm of Lake Charlevoix every day. The ferry received notoriety in 1936 when Ripley's Believe it or Not featured former captain Sam Alexander for travelling 15,000 miles while never being more than 1000 feet from his home.

OPPOSITE PAGE BOTTOM: The 110-feet-long *Keweenaw Star* returns to Round Lake after a sunset cruise on Lake Charlevoix and Lake Michigan.

ABOVE: Inside one of the exclusive boathouses along Round Lake.

RIGHT: In 1982, a group called Keep Charlevoix Beautiful launched "Operation Petunia." Every year, hundreds of volunteers show up on the Thursday before Memorial Day to plant petunias along the five miles of roadway from city limit to city limit.

ABOVE AND LEFT: The St Marys cement plant was built on South Point along Lake Michigan in 1967.

OPPOSITE PAGE: Before the upper channel (near the bottom of the photo) was cut through in 1869, Old River (above the large concrete slab) was the only access between Round Lake and Lake Charlevoix. Up until 1983 a railroad trestle and swing bridge crossed the channel just below the building at lower left. On the horizon are the faint outlines of North Fox and South Fox Islands.

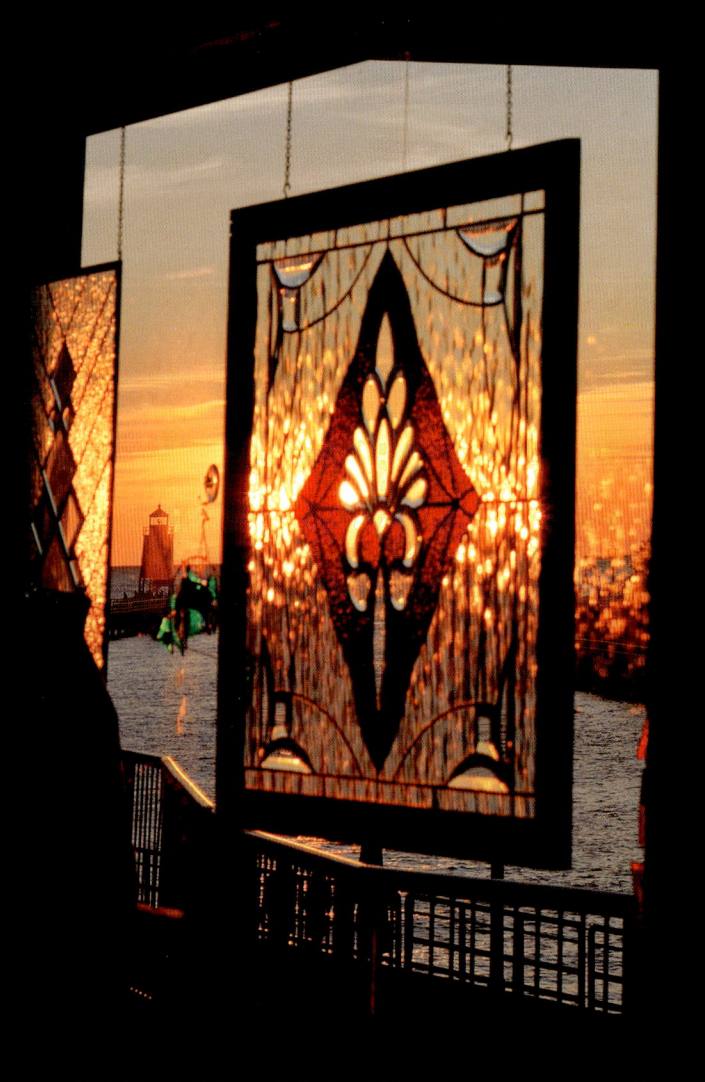

ABOVE: The window in an establishment overlooking the the Pine River channel.

RIGHT: The 257-feet-long, 43-feet-wide *Yorktown* cruise ship anchors in Round Lake. The *Yorktown* is able to maneuver in small ports that are inaccessible to larger ships because it only has a nine-foot draft underneath the water.

BRIDGE STREET

Something magical takes hold from the moment you arrive here. The charming and colorful downtown with its buzzing atmosphere overlooks the huge green lawn of East Park and picturesque, once landlocked Round Lake.

Bridge Street, just four blocks long, is a magnet for visitors and locals alike. But don't let the size fool you. The tree-shaded sidewalks are packed with an array of restaurants, candy and fudge shops, ice cream parlors, pastry shops, book stores and other establishments.

Many of buildings that line the historic downtown, even some that date back to 1885, are painted in every color of the rainbow. And how different would this town be if it didn't leave a three-block gap to take advantage of the waterfront view.

We are lucky that Charlevoix hasn't lost its small-town feeling and warm hospitality. Bridge Street welcomes you with open arms and what better place to shop or eat and watch the village bustle with activity above the delightful lake setting below.

CHARLEVOIX THE BEAUTIFUL II

The annual Charlevoix Street Legends Classic Car Show rolls into town in July. The car club was formed by local car enthusiasts in 1992.

BRIDGE STREET

LEFT AND BELOW: Sunrise along Bridge Street is always quiet and peaceful.

OPPOSITE PAGE: With so much to see and do, Bridge Street has people going in all directions.

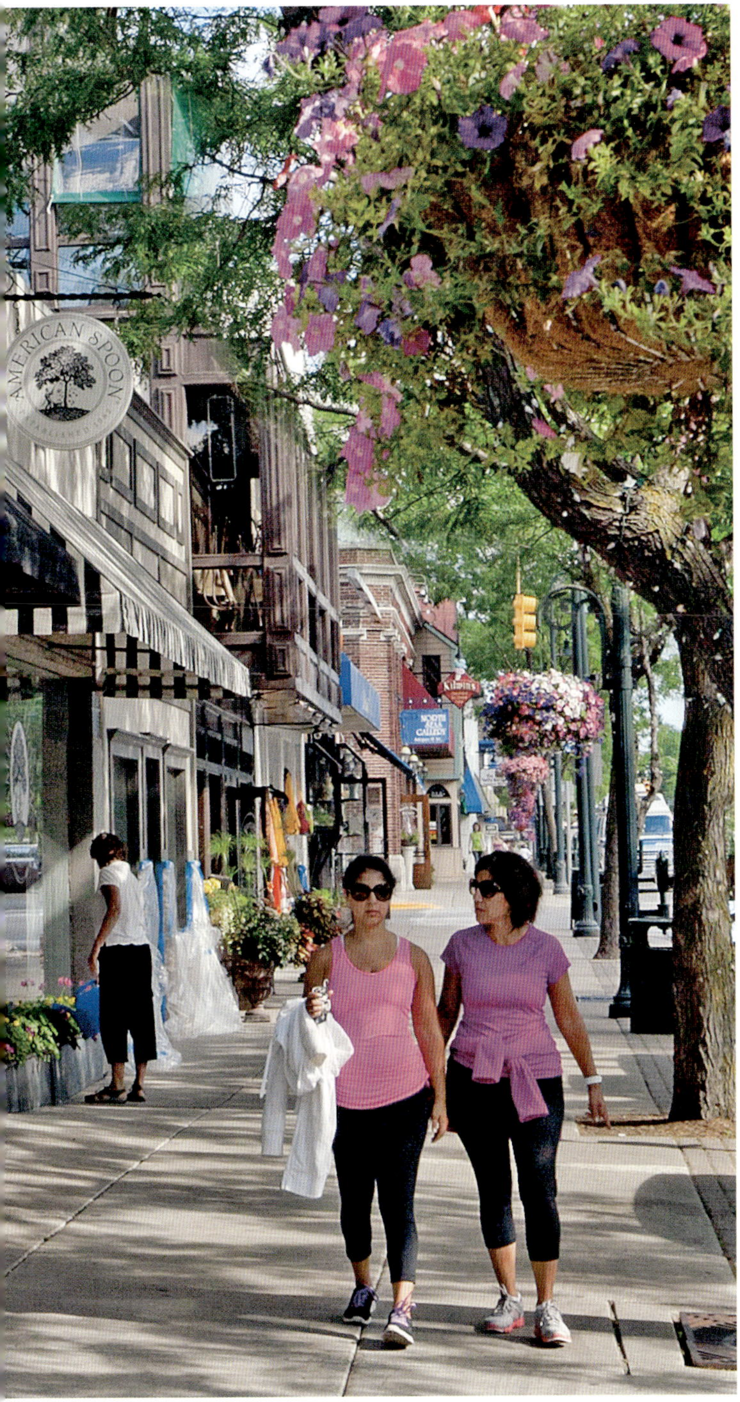
AMERICAN SPOON

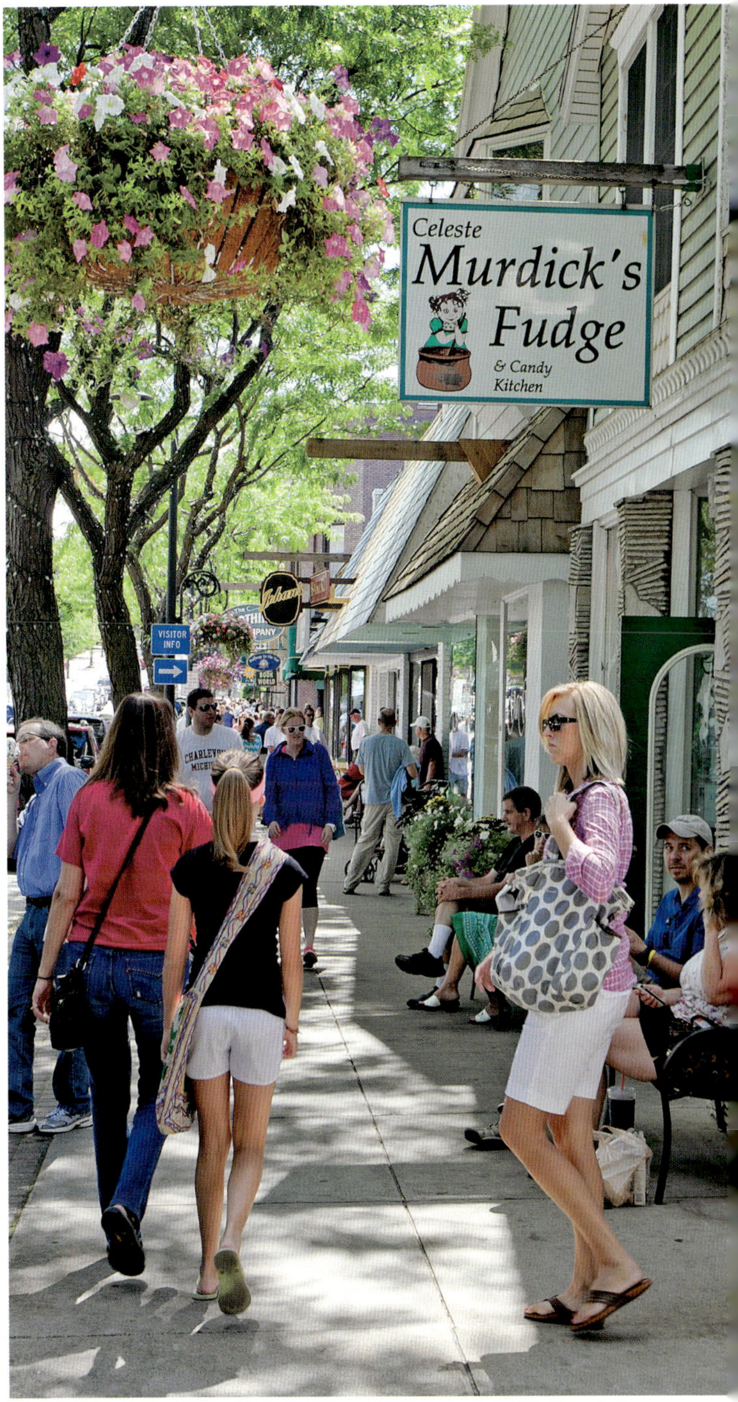
Celeste
Murdick's
Fudge
& Candy
Kitchen
VISITOR
INFO

LEFT AND OPPOSITE PAGE: Apple Fest is Charlevoix's fall harvest celebration with over thirty types of apples and other fall favorites such as pumpkins, jam, maple syrup, squash and cider. Bundle up!

BELOW: At sunrise, Bridge Street is bejeweled in its warm glow.

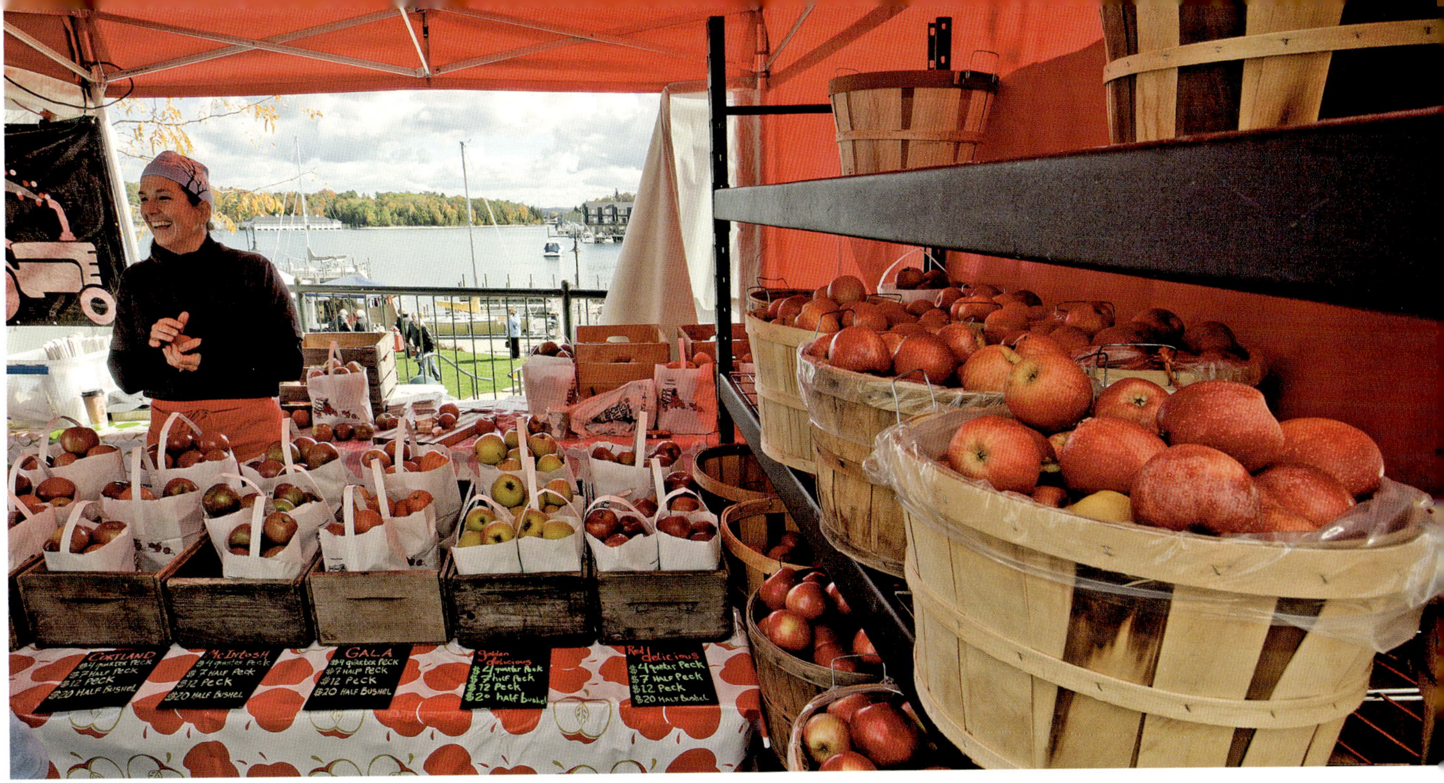
CORTLAND
$4 quarter PECK
$7 HALF PECK
$12 PECK
$20 HALF BUSHEL
McINTOSH
$4 quarter PECK
$7 HALF PECK
$12 PECK
$20 HALF BUSHEL
GALA
$4 quarter PECK
$7 HALF PECK
$12 PECK
$20 HALF BUSHEL
Golden delicious
$4 quarter Peck
$7 half Peck
$12 Peck
$20 half bushel
Red delicious
$4 quarter Peck
$7 HALF Peck
$12 Peck
$20 HALF Bushel

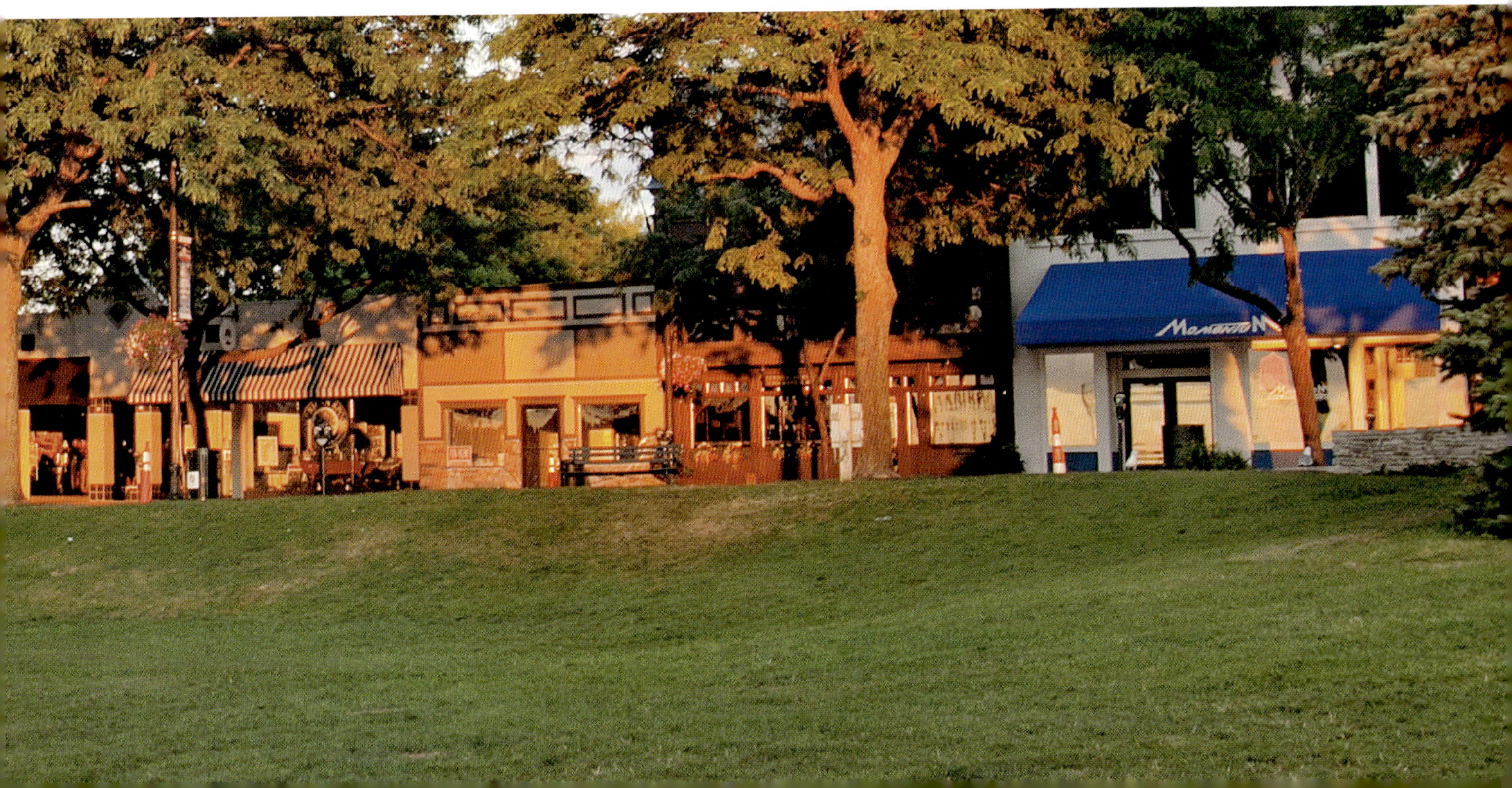

There is no shortage of fudge along Bridge Street.
PAGE 42-43: The Charlevoix Street Legends Classic Car Show.

The Farmers Market is held along Bridge Street every Thursday during the summer and fall.

Charlevoix Yacht Basin

As you walk or ride down Bridge Street, you can't help but take a peek at the spectacular view overlooking East Park and Round Lake. Where else can you find a downtown perched over such a scenic waterfront gem?

The beautifully kept grassy park is home to many events and is an ideal place to picnic or relax while watching sailboats and yachts bobbing in the harbor.

Often called the best natural harbor on Lake Michigan, Round Lake is surrounded by fancy boathouses and terraced ridges covered with elegant homes. When the day is coming to a close, many people take a peaceful stroll along the marina when the warm light makes this setting even more impressive.

LEFT: If you have kids, bring a towel because they will enjoy running around the Fountain of Youth.

OPPOSITE PAGE: The Charlevoix Waterfront Art Fair, the second oldest juried art fair in Michigan, is held in East Park every August. The pond at the bottom of the photo is a fully functioning trout habitat with rapids and waterfalls.

Members of the Charlevoix Street Legends Classic Car Club find a prime spot on the eve of the annual show.

CHARLEVOIX YACHT BASIN

The steamships and schooners that once hoisted their anchors in Round Lake have been replaced by ferries, sailboats and yachts.

ABOVE: The schooner *Inland Seas* returns to Charlevoix. While most of this schooner's activities take place in the Grand Traverse Bay region, what better place to drop anchor than Charlevoix?

Memorial Bridge

Memorial Bridge is Charlevoix's most notable landmark. The bridge opened to traffic in 1949 and is the sixth bridge built over the Pine River channel. The first bridge was just a small wooden footbridge built in 1859 before the river was dredged in 1870 to allow the passage of larger vessels. This bridge was dedicated as the Charlevoix Memorial Bridge to honor the men of Charlevoix who gave their lives during World War II.

The double-leaf bascule drawbridge opens for boaters every half hour and provides entertainment for those who gather to watch the boats flow between the two raised halves. Even locals never seem to get tired of watching the passing spectacle.

Charlevoix's annual "Little But Mighty Bridge Walk" held on Labor Day is a fun poke at the Mighty Mackinac Bridge Walk. But instead of a grueling five-mile trek over the Mackinac Bridge, participants can reach the finish line in a hop, skip and jump.

MEMORIAL BRIDGE

BELOW: The *Yorktown*, built in Florida in 1988 and renovated in 2009, maneuvers through the channel and slips away under the cover of darkness.

CHARLEVOIX THE BEAUTIFUL II

Charlevoix Lighthouse

With much fanfare, the lighthouse went through a historical restoration when the white tower was painted red in 2009. At the time, most people didn't know that the tower was red from 1914 to 1968 and only remembered it being white.

The original wooden tower was built in 1885 on the north pier. It was moved to the south pier in 1911 and was replaced by the current steel lighthouse in 1948. But the black lantern housing is from the 1885 light.

The pyramidal lighthouse is surprisingly very photogenic, thanks to the sleek silhouette of the south pier and vibrant sunsets.

CHARLEVOIX THE BEAUTIFUL II

CHARLEVOIX LIGHTHOUSE

The Big Dipper rises over the Lighthouse after midnight.

CHARLEVOIX LIGHTHOUSE

CHARLEVOIX THE BEAUTIFUL II

BEACHES

Whatever experience you are seeking, Charlevoix has a beach for you. It's where you can enjoy the rhythmic sound of waves, a gentle summer breeze, the call of a seagull and the laughter of children.

Lake Michigan Beach is a favorite spot to watch the stunning sunsets over the great lake. Children play on playground equipment while adults soak up the sun on the sugar sand beach or hunt for Petoskey stones along the shoreline.

Depot Beach is located on the west shore of Lake Charlevoix near the historic Charlevoix Train Depot. Further south on Lake Charlevoix is Ferry Beach. Both beaches usually have calmer and warmer water than Lake Michigan Beach.

If you are looking for a remote out of the way beach, the Lake Michigan shoreline along the Mount McSauba nature area is the place. A trailhead takes you to windswept dunes that roll down to a sandy beach.

OPPOSITE PAGE TOP: The Charlevoix Fisheries Research Station along Lake Michigan Beach glows at sunset.

OPPOSITE PAGE BOTTOM: Depot Beach on the east side of Charlevoix is a good launching point for kayaks because of the calm surf and water.

RIGHT: Lake Michigan Beach is just a short walk from downtown.

BELOW: The beach north of the lighthouse leads all the way to North Point in the far distance.

The Venetian Festival Parade features the reigning queen with her court (above) and kids on bikes and scooters (opposite page).

Venetian Festival

What began in 1930 as a parade of boats with candle-lit paper lanterns to celebrate the end of the sailing regattas has blossomed into a weeklong celebration in late July that draws thousands of visitors.

Charlevoix's signature event includes parades, carnival rides, music, games, fireworks and private parties galore. No other festival is more lively, colorful or fun-loving. Yearly traditions like this provide a legacy of fun and anticipation.

The magical boat parade in Round Lake is still the heart of the Venetian Festival. After darkness falls, the water in the harbor begins to sparkle from the reflective glow of the illuminated boats as they circle Round Lake while fireworks light up the sky.

Cottages and Gardens

Polished and sophisticated to rustic and casual, you can find your very own favorite from Charlevoix's collection of homes and cottages with a character only time can improve.

Whether it's a picket fence aged to perfection or a birdhouse tucked among the flowers and trees, there is something essentially charming about a simple cottage surrounded by a decorously gentle landscape. From early spring until late fall, something is blooming and adding splashes of color to the immaculate gardens.

One thing about living in an old cottage is discovering its individuality and eccentricities. For some it's a place where they raised a family, for others it's a retreat from a place far away from Charlevoix.

COTTAGES AND GARDENS

PAGE 4 AND 74: The Harsha House was built in 1891 by Charlevoix community leader Horace Harsha. His granddaughter, Ann Harsha, donated the Queen Anne-styled house to the Charlevoix Historical Society in 1979 and it is now a museum filled with photographs, documents, books, artifacts and local history.

RIGHT: Earl Young left a legacy when he built twenty-three stone houses affectionately named Mushroom Houses due to their wave-lined roofs.

RIGHT: A meticulously cared for harborside garden on Round Lake.

COTTAGES AND GARDENS

Not much has changed along this tranquil setting on the Belvedere Club's lakeside bluff over 135 years. It can take you back the way life used to be, to when it moved at a slower pace. The peace and quiet at sunrise are unmatched at any other time of day.

OPPOSITE PAGE: Perched on a high bluff overlooking Round Lake, the vibrant colors and whimsical ornate touches of this house draw your attention.

The Castle

One of the most unique and interesting places found in Northern Michigan is historic Castle Farms. Architect Arthur Heun's design was inspired by the ancient stone barns and Renaissance castles found in Normandy, France.

Loeb Farm was constructed in 1918 by Albert Loeb, vice president of Sears, Roebuck and Company, as a working dairy farm to showcase livestock and new farm equipment that was sold by his company.

The farm closed in 1927 and was used as a storage facility until John van Haver bought the property in 1962 and turned it into an art gallery and artist's studio. After van Haver sold the castle to Arthur and Erwina Reibel in 1969, it became a music theater and summer concert venue. From 1976-1993, Castle Farms played host to over 100 rock bands.

Linda Mueller became the fourth owner in 2001 and tastefully restored the castle while preserving its old-world charm.

Today, Charlevoix's very own fairy tale castle, with its magnificent soaring stone towers, archways, cobblestone walkways and gorgeous gardens is open for tours, celebrations, art fairs, and is one of the Midwest's premier wedding locations.

ABOVE: The Knight's Courtyard is used for weddings and other events. Inside the stately reception room you will find the perfect mix of the castle's historic past and modern-day elegance.

OPPOSITE PAGE: You can play a giant game of chess or lawn croquet while admiring the castle in the distance.

LEFT: This quiet little pond next to the castle with whimsical bridges and stricking reflections is an ideal spot to just get away.

Summer Resort Associations

With three historic summer resort associations, Charlevoix has long been a cherished vacation refuge to rest the body and mind. They are places time forgot. Everywhere you turn you see memories of days past. The history seems endless.

Many summer guests made the journey through the Great Lakes on passenger steamships in the late 1800s. Others arrived at one of the two train depots that served the Belvedere and Chicago Clubs. While early members stumbled upon these serene settings and created peaceful summer havens, those who followed were captivated by their unspoiled antiquity and knew to leave well enough alone. The original buildings continue to grace these communities and club traditions are passed down from one generation to the next.

The elite Belvedere Club, formed by a group of Baptists from Kalamazoo, Michigan in 1878, was Charlevoix's first summer resort association. Nestled within a shady spread of ancient trees and immense lawns, members spend time with family and experience

LEFT AND BELOW: The Chicago Club's clubhouse was built in 1881. As you enter the building, the spirit of the place takes over and the charm and authenticity resonate with the history of the past.

the rhythm of the long summer days. Ordinary life seems a million miles away and one can simply surrender to sitting in a wicker chair as the beauty draws them in and holds them under its spell.

On the other side of the upper channel, members of the First Congregational Church of Chicago who came north on a fishing expedition in 1880 returned and formed the Chicago Club in 1881. With many old enchanting cottages tucked on a gentle slope overlooking two lakes, it's a community that has not, over time, lost its old-fashioned charm.

Further south along Lake Charlevoix is the Sequanota Club formed in 1902 by professors and preachers from Illinois. The twenty-two cottages were built to take advantage of the waterfront view. It is where you can find seclusion down a long, windy road far away from town but close to the water.

Families return to these resorts generation after generation to reunite with lifelong friends. The past is all around you, and the wonderful thing is, it's still alive.

PAGE 92: Belvedere Club. This walkway meanders along a peaceful stretch atop a lakefront bluff lined with cottages and towering trees.

PAGE 93: Under an umbrella of autumn colors with a carpet of leaves, the Sequanota Club's rustic bridge only becomes more enchanting. The grounds have remained relatively unchanged and echo the days of long ago.

ABOVE AND RIGHT: Cabanas along the Belvedere Club's private beach bask in the sunrise glow. It is easy to understand why one returns summer after summer.

ABOVE: For many who pass through the Belvedere Club gatehouse entrance, it's a place they feel most at home in the world.
OPPOSITE PAGE TOP: A trip down Belvedere Avenue suddenly reveals a glimpse of the club's sheltered bayou and boathouses.
OPPOSITE PAGE BOTTOM: It is the small detail, the delicate play of light and shadow, that ultimately captures your heart.

Back Roads

In the course of a day, one can disengage from the hustle and bustle and discover the countryside surrounding Charlevoix. Almost instantly, you're in places that have changed very little over time

The roads curve gracefully through vast stretches of landscape dotted with ponds, fruit trees, farmland, wildflowers and forests, and you begin to wonder if it will ever end. Rabbits and deer bound over the open fields. At every dip, crest and turn of the road, the view changes.

Fall is a tranquil period when the sounds of the forest echo around you. Mother Nature takes her paintbrush and promises to put on a brilliant show. Every country road becomes a leaf-peeping excursion into fall colors ranging from a subtle yellow to brilliant orange to flaming red.

LEFT: Otis Pottery is a friendly place full of handcrafted wood-fired stoneware.

BELOW: Stonehedge Gardens is a unique home and garden shop in an intimate cottage setting.

BELOW: Bolt's Farm grows more than 300 tons of pumpkins each year

ABOVE: The Greensky Hill Old Cemetery rests in a tranquil yet eerie woodsy setting behind the church.

LEFT: The Greensky Hill Church was founded in 1844 by Peter Greensky, a Chippewa chief, who came to the area to start his own mission. The log church was constructed in the 1850s out of lumber carried by canoe from Traverse City.

PAGE 98 AND ABOVE: Fed by a series of natural streams, the Jordan Valley Trout Pond is surrounded by a peaceful rural setting. The picturesque reflections of the original 1800s barns can be captivating.

LEFT: Examples of rural Americana are found along the roadsides.

OPPOSITE PAGE: Experience the magic of autumn in Northern Michigan.

BEYOND CHARLVOIX

Charlevoix's location makes it a perfect starting point to discover why Northern Michigan is summer living at its best.

You can choose to discover the other harbor towns along Lake Michigan and Lake Charlevoix or head inland to the sleepy and slow-paced villages that look the same as they did 100 years ago. Or you can hop in a boat and there is almost no limit to where you can go including several nearby islands.

Ernest Hemingway spent his first 22 summers with his family in Northern Michigan near Petoskey and called this area a "priceless place." You can follow his footsteps when you visit Horton Bay, Petoskey and Bay View.

Another way to explore the area is via the 26-mile Little Traverse Wheelway, a paved path from Charlevoix to Harbor Springs along the shoreline and wetlands.

ABOVE: With 56 miles of shoreline, Lake Charlevoix (the large lake at the top of the photo) was voted America's second-most beautiful lake by USA Today readers. Round Lake (the tiny lake) flows into Lake Michigan at bottom.
OPPOSITE PAGE: Driving directions on a sign at Sturgeon River Pottery near Petoskey.

Harbor Springs

Sheltered along the north shore of Little Traverse Bay is the picturesque village of Harbor Springs. Thousands of years ago, glaciers carved the deep harbor and grand ridges, creating the natural beauty that makes Harbor Springs a popular destination.

The village of Little Traverse was established in 1858 as a trading post and quickly became a summer destination for passenger ships and trains in the 1870s. Many well-known wealthy families like the Fords, Upjohns, Gambles (of Proctor & Gamble), and Offields (of Wrigley Gum) built summer cottages here.

Today, Harbor Springs has a quaint but upscale downtown near the harbor, the same scenic beauty and is host to many events and festivals. Outdoor enthusiasts can enjoy golf, skiing, biking and sailing or just hang out in one of the downtown parks or beaches and watch glamorous yachts and sailboats skim across the harbor.

ABOVE: The Little Traverse Lighthouse, built in 1886, is located at the tip of private Harbor Point and can only be photographed from the shore. The original fog bell tower in front of the lighthouse was built in 1896.

LEFT: The view from the bluff looks over the village of Harbor Springs and the harbor.

Petoskey

Petoskey is a delightful resort town overlooking Little Traverse Bay that has been a popular vacation spot since the horse and buggy days. The town was named "Petoskey" in honor of Chief Ignatius Petosegay in 1879.

The historic downtown Gaslight District attracts locals and visitors alike. The smell of homemade fudge still infiltrates the downtown areas as it did over a century ago.

Petoskey inspired Ernest Hemingway's first novel, *Torrents of Spring*, when he lived there during the winter of 1919-20.

Along the beaches around Little Traverse Bay you may find a Petoskey Stone, a 350-million-year-old fossilized coral souvenir to take home. The "sunburst" hexagon patterns make them easy to identify, especially when they are wet.

ABOVE: The Francis Solanus Indian Mission Church was built in 1859 and may be the oldest building in Petoskey.

RIGHT: The Petoskey pierhead is a popular place to hang out and have fun during the summer.

BAY HARBOR

Bay Harbor is an exclusive four-season resort built on the scarred remains of a massive cement plant. Shorty after the factory was demolished in 1994, the barrier between the huge crater that remained and Lake Michigan was removed allowing 2.5 billion gallons of water to form a new harbor within 24 hours.

With a deep harbor, marina, beaches, world-class golf, an equestrian club and a village full of shops and restaurants, Bay Harbor is lakeside luxury at its finest.

ABOVE: The turn-of-the-century style Inn at Bay Harbor stands along Little Traverse Bay.

BOYNE CITY

Boyne City is nestled on the southeast end of Lake Charlevoix about twenty minutes from Charlevoix.

First settled in 1856, Boyne City has earned a reputation as a great area to live and visit. It's a place where you can get lost in nature and stay connected to civilization if you choose. Boyne City has miles of shoreline, a boat marina, world-class golf, and a quaint downtown. Nearby Boyne Mountain, with views of Lake Charlevoix, is one of Michigan's best ski resorts.

ABOVE: The Boyne City boat marina is situated on the shore of Lake Charlevoix with easy access to Lake Michigan.

HORTON BAY

Horton Bay is a little village clinging to existence on the north shore of Lake Charlevoix between Boyne City and Charlevoix. As a youth, Ernest Hemingway spent his summers at the family cottage on nearby Walloon Lake but was a frequent visitor to Horton Bay where he preferred to hunt, fish and swim. The area became the inspiration for several of his famous "Nick Adams" short stories. Hemingway also married his first wife in 1921 in the town's church.

The general store (left) was built in June 1876, the same year and month as Custer's Last Stand at the Battle of the Little Big Horn.

BAY VIEW

Bay View is an elegant summer resort association nestled on a natural terrace that cascades down to the shoreline along Little Traverse Bay. The community is known for its charming Victorian gingerbread-style cottages, some of which are still owned by descendants of the founding families.

Twenty simple cottages and several community buildings were built by 1877 and followed by another 125 cottages, a hotel and a chapel within ten years. Bay View now has more than 440 cottages, two historic inns, thirty community buildings and a post office.

While he was living in Petoskey, a young Ernest Hemingway would often escape to the privacy of Evelyn Hall, a women's dormitory unoccupied in the winter.

Other Photo Books By Mike Barton

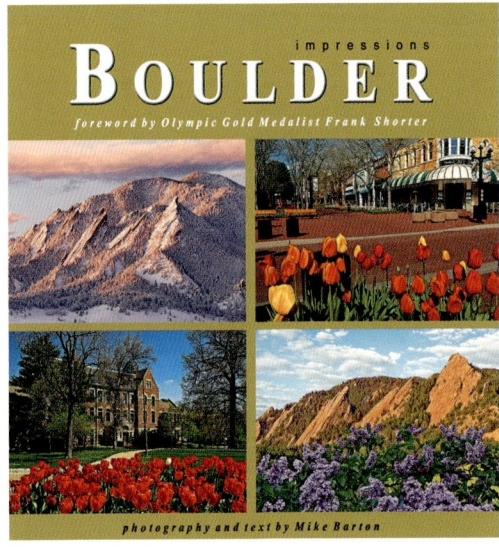
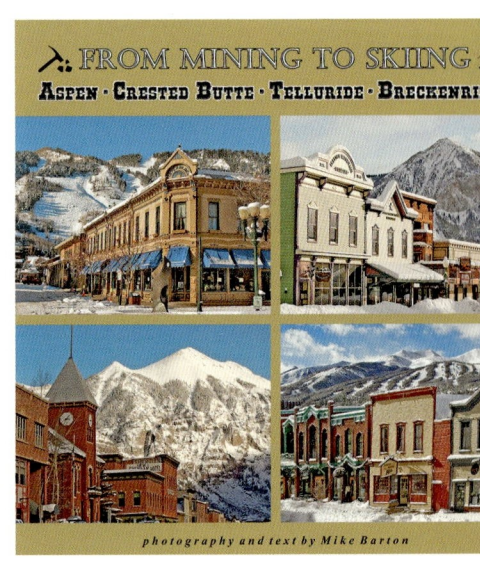
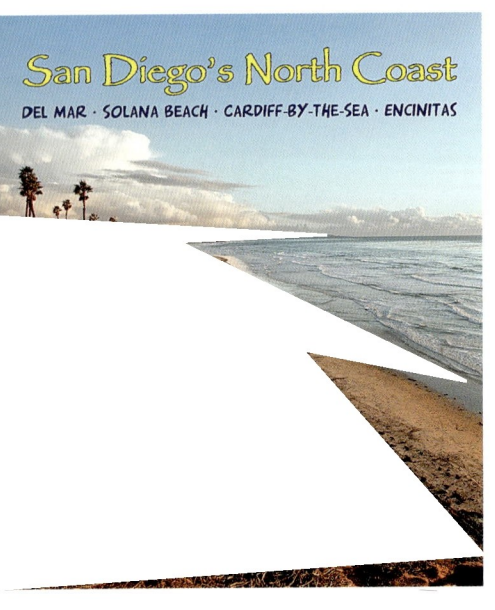
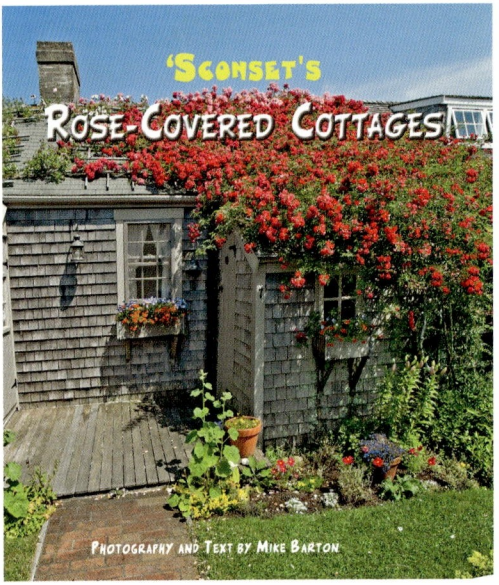
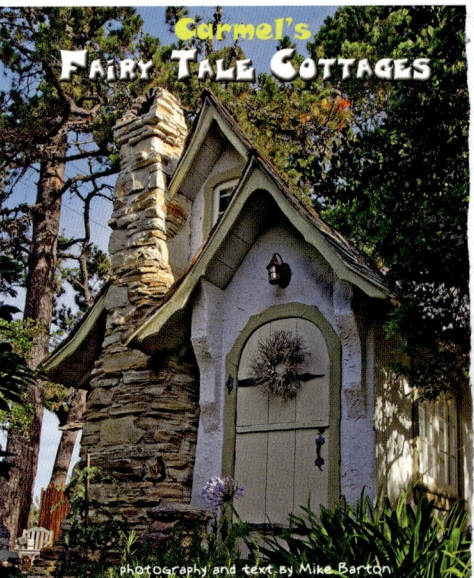

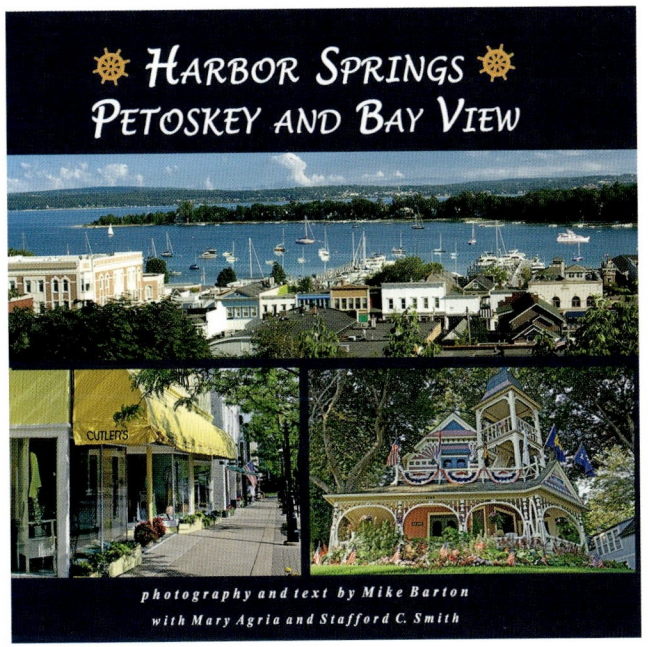
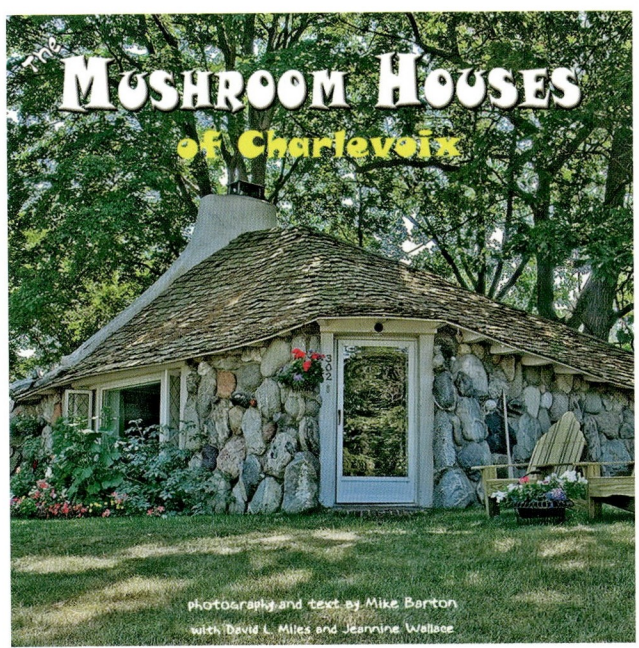

About the Photographer

Mike Barton is a landscape photographer from Solana Beach, California. A native of Michigan, Mike moved to sunny California after graduating from Michigan State and began to photograph the Pacific coast. Michigan is a great place to "be from."

Photography became a true passion when he moved to Boulder, Colorado where he honed his skills photographing in the Colorado mountains.

Mike continues to visit Charlevoix every summer as he has since his parents retired here in the early 1990s. He began working on the second edition of *Charlevoix the Beautiful* in 2009.

Many people comment on the vibrant colors that Mike is able to bring out in his photographs. This requires returning to the same place over and over until the light and other conditions are just right. A photo can be taken of the same location on different days and the clouds, colors, waves and reflections can vary dramatically.

His photos are on display in Charlevoix, Boulder and Carmel-by-the-Sea. To see more of Mike's work, please visit his website: www.mikebartonphoto.com.